King James Only Revised Dispensationalism Dismantled

KING JAMES ONLY
REVISED DISPENSATIONALISM
DISMANTLED

2nd Edition

David E. Walker

© COPYRIGHT 2020 DAVID E. WALKER

SECOND EDITION © COPYRIGHT 2023 DAVID E. WALKER

All rights reserved. No part of this book may be reproduced or used in any manner without the prior written permission of the copyright owner, except for the use of brief quotations in a book review.

Scripture quotations are from the Authorized King James Version.

ISBN: 979-8-8705-9678-5

Revised 2/1/24

CONTENTS

Introduction vii

1 A Little Background 1

2 Salvation Under the Law 15

3 Calvinism Contaminations 19

4 Tribulation Salvation 31

5 Truth Misapplied 47

Conclusion 53

Bibliography 55

Scripture Index 63

INTRODUCTION

Most believers raised in churches that contend for the King James Bible as the infallible word of God are familiar with 2 Timothy 2:15 and the idea of dispensationalism. In fact, most Bible believers are so familiar with their Scofield Reference Bibles they can tell you which side of the page a certain passage is on from memory. For many Bible believers, dispensationalism, as a theological system, answers *problem passages* that clearly teach salvation by means other than **"by grace…through faith"** in the finished work of Jesus Christ (Ephesians 2:8). At the same time, many King James Only (KJO) believers are unsure if there are differences in salvation under the various dispensations. Their pastors may not emphasize or teach these distinctions, or they may have fallen prey to KJO preachers and authors who teach salvation is the same in all dispensations. Some of these authors have been teaching this faulty dispensational view for years, while others have more recently modified to this position.

This booklet will briefly trace the development of dispensationalism as it relates to salvation in different dispensations. Evidence will be given proving that the dispensationalism taught by many KJO preachers and authors is nothing more than a revised dispensational position rooted in Calvinism. The faulty ideas of this revised position will be dismantled by critiquing their major arguments and examining their books in light of *the* Book.

A Little Background

Progressive Revelation

Anyone familiar with church history understands the truth of progressive revelation: that we know more about the Bible now than the church did in the first few centuries (see Psalm 119:99). Sometimes this is glossed over by reformed theologians attempting to discredit dispensational theology on the grounds that dispensational teaching was not voluminous until the nineteenth century. They claim dispensationalism is a modern movement and thus invalid. This is done by ignoring documented facts showing "historical references to that which eventually systematized into dispensationalism,"[1] pretending early church fathers like Justin Martyr (110–165), Irenaeus (130–200), and Clement of Alexandria (150–220) did not make any dispensational divisions. However, church fathers like Tertullian (160–220), Hippolytus (170–235),

---

[1] Charles C. Ryrie, *Dispensationalism*, rev. ed. (Chicago: Moody Press, 1995), 63.

and Cyril of Jerusalem (313–386) taught the dispensational truth that Israel would be restored and revived.[2] And pre–Darby theologians like Pierre Poiret (1646–1719), John Edwards (1637–1716), and Isaac Watts (1674–1748) made clear dispensational partitions.[3] Anti-dispensationalists have to disregard these facts as well as other abundant evidence showing clear pre–Darby "dispensational systems" in the writings of Samuel Hutchinson (1590–1667), Henry More (1614–87), and William Penn (1644–87) to name a few.[4]

Dispensationalism, as a theological movement, arose within premillennialism and the fundamentalist movement.[5] It was a distinctive part of the last phase of the Philadelphia Church Age (Revelation 3:7–13) and, as critics correctly point out, was "dependent in many ways on the King James translation of the Bible."[6] The dispensationalism of this period (1878–1940s) was primarily an *English* Bible study movement with an emphasis on *belief* in the Bible. The many Bible conferences and revivals of this time did not originate from seminaries or scholar's academic dissertations. They arose from a hunger to learn the Bible. And the Bible most people had, read, and believed was the Authorized Version (AV). The fruits of this period were not just personal light for the believer, but light for the world. Many Bible institutes with

---

[2] James C. Morris, *Ancient Dispensational Truth: Refuting the Myth that Dispensationalism is New* (Taos, NM: Dispensational Publishing House, Inc., 2018), 50–62.

[3] Ryrie, *Dispensationalism*, 65–67.

[4] William C. Watson, *Dispensationalism before Darby* (Silverton, OR: Lampion Press, 2015), 119, 124–25.

[5] George M. Marsden, *Fundamentalism and American Culture* (New York: Oxford, 2006), 48–62.

[6] Ben Witheringon III. *The Problem with Evangelical Theology* (Waco: Baylor University Press, 2005), 95.

a dispensational emphasis rose from this movement and pushed missions and evangelism way beyond what other groups were doing at the time.

But as the lights of the Philadelphia period went out, the Bible institute and missionary movement gave way to the dead seminary movement. Dispensational teachers aspired to be *scholars* and as such, did not retain the simple honest belief in the word of God. The revised period of dispensationalism saw a rise in criticism of the King James text, and, with the publication of the *New Scofield Reference Bible* in 1967, "a toning down of Scofield's material."[7] The revised period of dispensationalism dropped the torch of honesty and belief in the Bible. Instead, their scholarship got the best of them, and they began apologizing for the obvious implications of dispensationalism—namely that people were saved differently under the different dispensations.

> Scofield and Chafer (and they are not alone) left an impression that salvation comes in various ways. These were unfortunate statements. It may be argued that they were said early in the debate and were not thought through well. It must also be admitted that the dispensationalism of today is not the same as the dispensationalism of Scofield, Chafer, Walvoord, and other early writers. There has been additional study and revision.[8]

---

[7] Todd R. Mangum and Mark S. Sweetnam, *The Scofield Bible* (Colorado Springs: Paternoster, 2009), 201.

[8] Larry R. Oats, "Salvation in Dispensationalism," *Frontline Magazine* 20, no. 4 (July/August 2010): 10–12, https://fbfi.org/wpcontent/uploads/2017/01/2010.08.FrontLine.pdf.

BIBLE-BELIEVING DISPENSATIONALISM

KJO Bible-believing dispensationalism, as a movement, was a reaction to this revised dispensationalism apostasy much like the fundamentalist movement was a counter to modernism. To the Bible believer, the logical conclusions of **"rightly dividing"** were only as good as the Bible itself. Inspiration was correctly understood to apply to an actual book that could be "studied" (2 Timothy 2:15)—the King James Authorized Version, not just the original manuscripts. This meant that "pastor popes who privately interpreted the scripture with their cute sayings"[9] could be challenged because the power was in the word of God, not the word of men. This further led to honestly approaching the Bible in humble belief as a student, not a scholar. The outcome was an ardent belief in dispensational salvation—that salvation conditions *are* different, regardless of what scholarship says or has said in the past.

The KJO movement and this brand of dispensationalism are inseparably linked. Unfortunately, some KJO preachers and authors today are espousing revised or normative dispensationalism. They side theologically with Bible correctors, assuming the distinguishing differences between Israel and the church are only ecclesiological (dealing with the church), or eschatological (dealing with prophecy), and not soteriological (dealing with salvation). In other words, they claim that even "under the Old Testament Law…salvation was available to the sinner…not by the works of

---

[9] Brian Donovan, "One Book Wrongly Divided…Twice," *Bible Believers' Bulletin* 43 (June 2019): 16.

the Law but by grace through faith."[10] They maintain, "in every age, salvation comes by faith and is offered and granted through grace."[11] These authors, by their own admission[12] and obvious absence of quoted source material, or very limited references in their books, are very careful not to name the KJO authors they are attempting to refute.[13] They piously profess to be "concerned with what is being taught, not with the men themselves."[14]

These authors are specifically targeting Bible believers who have either adopted the truths of dispensational salvation personally or have been taught these truths by their pastors. They are attempting to undermine true KJO dispensationalism and are in effect reverting back to revised dispensationalism (Ryrie, Pentecost, LaHaye, et al.) at worst, or classical dispensationalism (Scofield, Larkin, Haldeman, Blackstone, et al.) at best. These preachers and authors are advocating a KJO brand of revised dispensationalism—one that makes no distinction between salvation differences throughout the various ages of human history.

THE CLASSIC POSITION

Although classic dispensationalists failed to pinpoint and clarify the biblical truth of dispensational salvation, they bumped into it on

---

[10] James W. Knox, *The Law and Rightly Dividing the Word Reconsidered* (DeLand, FL: The Bible Baptist Church, 2009), 74.

[11] Douglas D. Stauffer and Andrew B. Ray, *One Book Rightly Divided Prophetic Edition* (Knoxville, TN: McCowen Mills Publishers & LTB Publications, 2018). 668.

[12] James W. Knox, *By Definition: A Readers Guide to the King James Bible* (DeLand, FL: The Bible Baptist Church of DeLand, 1996, 2013), 329.

[13] Dennis Corle, *What Salvation Is* (Claysburg, PA: Revival Fires! Publishing, 2015), 245–264.

[14] M.H. Tabb, *The Gap Theory* (Fort Walton Beach: Foundation Ministries, 1993), 17.

several occasions. C. I. Scofield's note on John 1:17 was the focus on what was referred to as "the two ways of salvation debate"[15] because it reflected the biblical idea that salvation is not the same in each dispensation:

> Law is connected with Moses and works; grace with Christ and faith...Law demands that blessings be earned; grace is a free gift...As a dispensation, grace begins with the death and resurrection of Christ (Rom. 3:24–26, 4:24–25). The point of testing is no longer legal obedience as the condition of salvation, but acceptance or rejection of Christ...[16]

Scofield's note in 1 John 3:7 likewise highlighted this salvation distinction, stating, "The righteous man under law became righteous by doing righteously; under grace he does righteously because he has been made righteous (Rom. 3:22, 10:3, note)."[17] The Scofield note under the Edenic Covenant said that covenants "condition life and salvation."[18] And the note under the Lord's Prayer clarified that it was "legal ground...under law forgiveness is conditioned upon a like spirit in us; under grace we are forgiven for Christ's sake."[19]

Although unorthodox on several points, E. W. Bullinger (1837–1913) correctly observed that the Law offered a righteousness

---

[15] Gordon Campbell, *Bible: The Story of the King James Version 1611–2011* (New York: Oxford University Press, 2010), 246.

[16] C. I. Scofield, ed., *Scofield Reference Bible* (New York: Oxford University Press, 1909), 1115.

[17] Ibid., 1323.

[18] Ibid., 5–6.

[19] Ibid., 1002.

based on works,[20] and others like Robert Milligan (1814–1875) stated that the Law

> served to preserve and to sustain in the world the then imperfectly developed scheme of justification by faith; so that, no doubt, hundreds and thousands of Jews were saved through its influence and instrumentality.[21]

Isaac M. Haldeman (1845–1933), otherwise known during his day as "the Dispensational Pastor,"[22] made a similar case, implying that Old Testament Jews under the Law were not saved by faith only, but by their works:

> In the Mosaic dispensation, God dealt according to man's work. In the Holy Ghost dispensation, He deals according to Christ's work. In the Mosaic dispensation, God dealt on the basis of Law. In the Holy Ghost dispensation. He deals on the basis of Grace. In the Mosaic dispensation, God said: "Do, and live." In the Holy Ghost dispensation, He says: "Live, and do." In the Mosaic dispensation, the Law brought a work for man to do. In the Holy Ghost dispensation, the gospel brings a Word for man to believe. In the Mosaic dispensation, all is summed up in a word of two letters, "Do." In the Holy Ghost dispensation, all is summed up in a word of four letters, "Done."[23]

---

[20] E. W. Bullinger, *The Companion Bible* (Grand Rapids: Kregel, 1990), 248.

[21] Robert Milligan, *An Exposition and Defense of the Scheme of Redemption,* 3rd rev. ed. (Cincinnati: R.W. Carroll & Co., 1869), 84.

[22] *Reese Chronological Encyclopedia of Christian Biographies* (Chattanooga: AMG, 2007), 667.

[23] I. M. Haldeman, *Friday Night Papers, the Second Coming, and other Expositions* (New York: Theo. Audel & Company, 1901), 169.

Even Scofield's protégé Lewis Sperry Chafer (1871–1952) in his classic systematic theology alluded to the biblical conclusion of clear salvation differences between the Old and New Testaments:

> A distinction must be observed here between just men of the Old Testament and those justified according to the New Testament. According to the Old Testament men were just because they were true and faithful in keeping the Mosaic Law. …Men were therefore just because of their own works for God, whereas New Testament justification is God's work for man in answer to faith (Rom. 5:1).[24]

Similar remarks by Chafer would later be challenged by five-point Calvinist theologians, causing him to emphatically deny ever teaching two ways of salvation.[25] Reflecting the consensus of reformed theology, in 1944, the Southern Presbyterian Church denounced dispensationalism on soteriological grounds:

> Dispensationalism rejects the doctrine that God has, since the Fall, but one plan of salvation for all mankind and affirms that God has been through the ages administering various and diverse plans of salvation for various groups.[26]

Chafer's revised and clarified position was that "the Law was never given as a means of salvation or justification,"[27] even though Romans 2:13 affirmed just the opposite. Much like Scofield and

---

[24] Lewis Sperry Chafer, *Systematic Theology*, vol. 7, *Doctrinal Summarization* (Grand Rapids: Kregel, 1976), 219.

[25] Ryrie, *Dispensationalism*, 108.

[26] PCA Historical Center, "1944 PCUS Report on Dispensationalism," accessed August 13, 2019, http://www.pcahistory.org/documents/pcus1944.html.

[27] Lewis Sperry Chafer, *Grace* (Philadelphia: The Sunday School Times, 1922), 113.

Larkin,[28] Chafer made the mistake of overlooking Romans 2:6–13, thus placing the truth of Galatians back into the period of the Old Testament. This horrendous error is repeated by KJO revised dispensationalists as well,[29] and is also supplemented by their misuse of Acts 13:39[30]—a verse given *after* the Crucifixion to explain New Testament salvation, and Galatians 3:21[31]—a verse magnifying New Testament justification and *imputed* righteousness over Old Testament Law keeping and *personal* righteousness. In the Old Testament, God judged by **"justifying the righteous"** (2 Chronicles 6:23), while in the New Testament, He **"justifieth the ungodly"** (Romans 4:5). The two are *not* the same.

REVISING THE CLASSIC VIEW

All professing dispensationalists would admit one of the main tenets of dispensationalism is "a clear, biblical distinction between Israel and the Church."[32] Revised dispensationalism, with its emphasis on salvation being the same in every dispensation, has muddled this clear distinction and aligned its teachings with reformed theology. The revised dispensationalist position that "the people of God [have] always been constituted by those who were joined to Him and to one another by grace through faith"[33] supports

---

[28] *Scofield Reference Bible,* 1245; Clarence Larkin, *Rightly Dividing the Word* (Glenside, PA: Rev. Clarence Larkin Est.,1920), 195.

[29] Knox, *The Law and Rightly Dividing the Word Reconsidered,* 63.

[30] Stauffer and Ray, *One Book Rightly Divided Prophetic Edition,* 280.

[31] Ibid., 697.

[32] Paul Richard Wilkinson, *For Zion's Sake* (Eugene: Wipf & Stock 2007), 13.

[33] Glenn R. Kreider, "What is Dispensationalism" in *Dispensationalism and the History of Redemption,* eds. D. Jeffrey Bingham and Glenn R. Kreider (Chicago: Moody, 2015), 24.

the replacement theology view that, "there is only one people of God"[34] and only one way of salvation after Adam's fall:

> Covenant theology traces this single covenant of grace throughout scripture. Although it was administered in various ways throughout the Old and New Testaments, covenant theologians agree on one crucial point — there is one covenant of grace (although a number of administrations) and thus only one way of salvation.[35]

The revised era of dispensationalism was mainly a "rearticulation and softening of former dispensational discussions such as the overstated dichotomy between law and grace."[36] This *adjusting* was done to expunge "the charge that [dispensationalists] teach different methods of salvation in different ages."[37] The clearest example of these revisions is seen in the *New Scofield Reference Bible* (now *The Scofield Study Bible III*), where repetitive statements are made affirming that, "there is only one basis of salvation, that is, by grace through faith."[38] Scofield's original note in John 1:17 was changed to teach salvation by faith in every age and the original remark in 1 John 3:7 on personal righteousness under the Law was removed altogether. The revision committee

---

[34] Norman Geisler, *Systematic Theology,* vol. 4, *Church, Last Things* (Bloomington, MN: Bethany House, 2005), 500.

[35] John H. Gerstner, *Wrongly Dividing the Word: A Critique of Dispensationalism, Second Edition,* (Morgan, PA: Soli Deo Gloria Publications, 2000), 305.

[36] Herbert W. Bateman IV, "Dispensationalism Yesterday and Today," in *Three Central Issues in Contemporary Dispensationalism,* ed. Herbert W Bateman IV (Grand Rapids: Kregel, 1999), 34.

[37] Clarence E. Mason Jr., *Dispensationalism Made Simple* (Glenside, PA: self-pub.), 1976, 14.

[38] C. I. Scofield, E. Schuyler English, and Doris W. Rikkers, eds., *The Scofield Study Bible III* (New York: Oxford, 2003), ix.

deleted the part of Scofield's note on the Edenic Covenant referring to a "condition of salvation" in the covenants. They also cleaned up the note on the Lord's Prayer and added additional notes proliferating the idea that "the method of salvation in OT and NT is the same."[39]

Charles Ryrie went to great lengths in his book *Dispensationalism* (originally *Dispensationalism Today*, 1966) to answer charges by reformed theologians, like Gerstner, who understandably observed that, "dispensationalists roundly assert that Old Testament people were saved by Christ, there is no way in their theological system they could be."[40] Gerstner, referencing the dispensational distinction between Israel and the church, rightly asked, "If these are two different people, how can they have the same salvation?"[41] Indeed, this is the crux of the matter and emphasizes the soteriological distinctions within dispensationalism.

THE *SCHOLAR'S* POSITION

Ryrie also devoted an entire chapter in his book refining the *dispensational scholar's* position on dispensational salvation. His summary is as follows:

> The basis of salvation in every age is the death of Christ; the requirement for salvation in every age is faith; the object of faith in every age is God; the content of faith changes in the various

---

[39] Ibid., 29.
[40] Gerstner, *Wrongly Dividing the Word*, 193.
[41] Ibid., 235.

dispensations...The basis of salvation is always the death of Christ; the means is always faith; the object is always God (though man's understanding of God before and after the incarnation is obviously different); but the content of faith depends on the particular revelation God was pleased to give at a certain time."[42]

Ryrie's unbiblical explanation is mirrored nearly word for word by KJO revised dispensationalists[43] and progressive fundamental Baptists.[44] They emphasize that "the difference has been in the object of faith," and salvation "always has been by grace, never by works."[45] Finding commonality with different groups who had "faith" no more proves "Moses was saved just like [we] are"[46] than Enoch was in the body of Christ because he was raptured!

There is ambiguity in the statements of KJO revised dispensationalists. Everyone knows many Old Testament saints had **"faith"** (Hebrews 11), but many do not know what their faith was *in*. In the Church Age, faith is equated with "trusting" and "believing" (Ephesians 1:12–13). This belief is *in* **"the righteousness of God without the law...which is by faith of Jesus Christ."** (Romans 3:21–22). A New Testament Christian is one who has **"believed in Jesus Christ"** (Galatians 2:16; Acts 16:1, 17:4, 12, 34, 18:8, 27; 1 Corinthians 15:11; etc.). In the Old Testament, the nation of Israel would all be considered "believers"

---

[42] Ryrie, *Dispensationalism*, 115, 121.

[43] Stauffer and Ray, *One Book Rightly Divided Prophetic Edition*, 55, 652, 668, 794.

[44] Paul Chappell, *Galatians: No Turning Back* (Lancaster, CA: Striving Together Publications, 2013), 54.

[45] M.H. Tabb, *Dispensational Salvation* (Ft. Walton Beach, FL: Foundation Ministries, 1991), 1–3.

[46] James Melton, "Understanding Dispensational Salvation", Bible Baptist Publications, accessed August 7, 2019, https://www.biblebaptistpublications.org/dispensationalsalvation.html.

(like in James 2:19) but they wouldn't be considered **"righteous"** (Deuteronomy 25:1) unless they did **"that which is lawful and right"** (Ezekiel 18:27). The "object" of their faith (see Ryrie's definition) was *not* "God" but their own works. Their **"works"** (Proverbs 24:12) showed whether or not they were **"obedient"** as God's people (see Exodus 24:7; Numbers 27:20; Deuteronomy 8:20; Isaiah 1:19, 24:24, etc.). A "believer" in the Church Age believes in the resurrection of Jesus Christ (see Acts 5:14) and consciously trusts in what Jesus Christ did on the cross, dying in his place (1 Corinthians 15:2–4). Old Testament saints under the Law trusted **"the righteousness which is of the law"** (Romans 10:5) while New Testament *believers* trust **"the righteousness which is of faith"** (Romans 10:6). Old Testament saints could not have **"the righteousness of God"** because this righteousness does not **"come by the law"** (Galatians 2:21), it comes by faith in Jesus:

> And be found in him, not having mine own righteousness, which is of the law, but that which is through the faith of Christ, the righteousness which is of God by faith: (Philippians 3:9)

A Clear Contrast

The contrast between **"grace"** and **"works"** is clear, distinct, and magnified in the following verse:

> And if by grace, then is it no more of works: otherwise grace is no more grace. But if it be of works, then is it no more grace: otherwise work is no more work. (Romans 11:6)

One KJO revised dispensationalist improvises the text of Romans 11:6 by actually changing it from **"no more of works"** to "not by works."[47] Another author, who changed his position on dispensational salvation, went from citing Romans 11:6 five times and teaching that **"no more of works"** indicated "that an element of works was involved at a prior time, but works is *no longer* involved,"[48] to omitting the verse both in his expanded edition[49] and his entirely new book by a similar title.[50] In a more recent book, the same author quoted Romans 11:6 to in an attempt to disprove faith and works under the Law.[51] But the context shows **"the election of grace"** (Romans 11:5) during the Church Age is simply illustrated by **"the election"** of Israel (Romans 11:28). Old Testament Jews during Elijah's day were *elect* "because of their works: they did not bow down to Baal."[52] People in the Church Age are *elect* **"by grace"** and it is **"through faith"** in Jesus Christ (Ephesians 2:8). The two are *not* the same salvation.

---

[47] Tabb, *Dispensational Salvation*, 2.

[48] Douglas D. Stauffer, *One Book Rightly Divided Second Edition* (Millbrook, AL: McCowen Mills Publishers, 1999, 2000). 47.

[49] Douglas D. Stauffer, *One Book Rightly Divided Expanded Edition* (Millbrook, AL: McCowen Mills Publishers, 1999, 2000, 2006).

[50] Stauffer and Ray, *One Book Rightly Divided Prophetic Edition.*

[51] Douglas D. Stauffer, *Tribulation Salvation: Jesus Still Saves* (Niceville, FL: McCowen Mills Publishers, 2020), 41.

[52] *Ruckman Reference Bible* (Pensacola: Bible Baptist Bookstore, 2009), 1501.

Salvation Under the Law

Basic Errors

KJO revised dispensationalists teaching about the Old Testament Law causes confusion instead of clarity. They claim no one could ever keep the Law[1] even though many verses state just the opposite – people in the Old Testament *did* keep the Law (Exodus 20:6, Deuteronomy 7:9; Joshua 22:2; Judges 2:17; 1 Kings 3:3, 1 Kings 11:34; 2 Kings 18:6; and 2 Chronicles 34:2). Next, KJO revised dispensationalists equate keeping the Law with living a sinless life[2] (which the Bible does not support). Then, they use a New Testament truth for the Church Age to explain Old Testament salvation (Galatians 2:16). Once this is done, any Old Testament teaching clearly showing justification by works (like the examples

---

[1] Stauffer and Ray, *One Book Rightly Divided Prophetic Edition,* 268, 353–4, 521, 621, 623, 703, 715.

[2] Knox, *The Law and Rightly Dividing the Word Reconsidered,* 37.

described in Ezekiel 18) must be twisted to keep their interpretation intact.

PHYSICAL LIFE OR SOUL?

The KJO revised dispensational position matches apostate dispensationalists who teach that keeping the Law was only "the means of temporal life" and did not affect their eternal salvation.[3] Pastor Donovan correctly refutes this idea, pointing out "what Christ Himself said about the meaning of dying in your sins in John 8:24."[4] When faced with this New Testament cross reference, KJO revised authors warn that "it is dangerous to superimpose New Testament doctrine on Old Testament teachings,"[5] yet they have no problem aggressively importing salvation by grace (a New Testament teaching) and justification by faith in the blood of Christ (a New Testament teaching) back into the entire Old Testament!

KJO revised dispensationalists also purposely avoid the issue that *works* determined whether a person was considered **"wicked"** or **"righteous."** They waste time on the double usage of the word **"soul"** and how it can "be used to identify and speak of man's physical being"[6] as simply a way of avoiding the plain truth of *faith-and-works* under the Old Testament Law. They do this while ignoring verses like Proverbs 19:16—**"He that keepeth the commandment keepeth his own soul."** The fact of the matter is,

---

[3] Ryrie, *Dispensationalism, 117.*

[4] Brian Donovan, "A Marriage for His Son," *Bible Believers' Bulletin* 41 (September 2017): 24.

[5] Stauffer and Ray, *One Book Rightly Divided Prophetic Edition,* 468.

[6] Ibid.

what an Old Testament saint *did* affected his eternal destiny (see **"doeth"** in Ezekiel 18:10-11, 14, 24, 27; Romans 10:5; and Galatians 3:12). If a man died **"wicked"** (Ezekiel 18:20, 21, 23, 24…) he went to hell (Psalm 9:17). Furthermore, if an Old Testament Jew died **"righteous"** he went to Abraham's bosom (Luke 16:22) and would later be redeemed by Christ's blood sacrifice. KJO revised dispensationalists attempt to turn the truth on its head by using Abraham's bosom as proof against faith-and-works under the Law:

> So I must ask you, if men before Calvary were saved in some way other than through the shed blood and finished work of the Lord Jesus Christ how is it that they could not go to heaven until the resurrected Christ took them there? Obviously, law keeping, or any other system of good works cannot get a man to heaven.[7]

A question in rebuttal would be, how can a man be saved "through the shed blood and finished work" of Christ before Christ was even born and began His work, let alone "finished" it? If the righteousness of God is a gift given to the believer by means of the Holy Spirit (Romans 5:17, 6:23; John 7:38–39; Ephesians 1:13, 4:30; 2 Corinthians 1:22 etc.), there is no way any Old Testament saint could have received this **"gift"** before it was given at Pentecost (Luke 24:49; Acts 2:38, 10:45, 11:17, 15:8–9). Are the KJO revised dispensationalists Bible believers or Calvinist sympathizers? Old Testament Jews under the Law never made a conscious choice to turn from their own self-righteousness and believe on Jesus' death, burial and resurrection (1 Corinthians 15:1–4) for their salvation. Instead, they knew they would be

---

[7] Knox, *The Law and Rightly Dividing the Word Reconsidered*, 272.

judged according to their personal **"righteousness"** and **"integrity"** (Psalm 7:8, 25:21, 26:11, 41:12, et al.). They were saved from hell, not based on their faith in the blood of Christ, but by their faith-and-works in keeping the Law while they were on the earth. They never would have been saved from hell and taken "to heaven" (Ephesians 4:8–9) had they not made it to Abraham's bosom in the first place!

CALVINISM CONTAMINATIONS

LOOKING FORWARD TO THE CROSS

To maintain their position, KJO revised dispensationalists must not only partner with Bible correctors (revised dispensationalists), but they must also collaborate with Calvinists. Once a concession is made for salvation by faith in the "finished work" of Christ (before Christ is ever born), other allowances must, of necessity, follow.

The theological reasons for the *saved the same* position of revised dispensationalists seems at first to have some biblical validity. After all, does not Scripture say, **"it is not possible that the blood of bulls and of goats should take away sins."** (Hebrews 10:4)? And, are we not **"redeemed…with the precious blood of Christ…who verily was foreordained before the foundation of the world"** (1 Peter 1:18–20)? If we are all sinners since Adam, regardless of dispensations, and all sinners are condemned to the same hell, is it not reasonable that the redemption for all sinners would be the same? According to this thinking, it does not matter *when* Jesus actually died, or what truth was dispensed in other ages. His blood is eternal, therefore "salvation is in Christ…[and] is eternal not dispensational."[1] Calvinist reformed theologians would agree. In fact, they insist that "believers of the Old Testament looked [to Jesus] and in him they trusted."[2] They contend that "the old covenant by which Israel was saved was the blood of Jesus Christ and faith in it, which technically is nothing less than the covenant of grace."[3]

The idea of looking forward to the cross for salvation in the Old Testament was partially insinuated in classical dispensationalism (see Scofield's note in Ezekiel 43:19), but the idea became an entrenched dogma of revised dispensationalism. You see, classic dispensationalists were good at highlighting distinctions between the various covenants, especially those differences between Israel and the Church. And, while they did not positively teach dispensational salvation, at least they presented the verses and formulated reasons that would logically lead to that conclusion. Revised dispensationalists, on the other hand, not only blur these differences, they dispute these teachings and indict classical dispensationalist views as "radical distinction[s]."[4]

---

[1] Corle, *What Salvation Is*, 264.

[2] Calvin Knox Cummings, "The Covenant of Grace," The Orthodox Presbyterian Church, accessed August 13, 2019, http:// www.opc.org/cce/covenant.html.

[3] Gerstner, *Wrongly Dividing the Word*, 312.

[4] Robert Dean Jr., "Essentials of Dispensational Theology," Dean Bible Ministries, accessed August 13, 2019, https://www.deanbibleministries.org/file-downloads /preview?path=Doctrines%252FEssentials_of_Dispensational_Theology.pdf.

J. Dwight Pentecost (1915–2014), taught that "salvation offered in the Old Testament was…accepted by faith, based on blood sacrifice, which sacrifices were the foreshadows of the true sacrifice to come."[5] R. B. Thieme Jr. taught that "the gospel existed in the form of promises of the coming Messiah (Gen. 3:15), who was depicted in the animal sacrifices."[6] Therefore, he concluded "the means of salvation in every dispensation has always been faith in the Lord Jesus Christ as He is revealed in that era."[7]

Many KJO revised dispensationalists still preach that Old Testament saints were saved by looking forward to the cross. This teaching is often referred to as "scarlet thread theology" because of the popularity of W. A. Criswell's sermon, *The Scarlet Thread through the Bible* (published in 1961). Covenant theologians likewise refer to this "vital thread running through the Old Testament"[8] and therefore teach "salvation has always been the same, namely by exercising faith in Christ."[9]

KJO revised dispensationalists often regurgitate these same Calvinistic ideas. And, when the question arises about whether or not Old Testament saints could have really understood Calvary, they answer, "it is impossible for us to discern what someone who has been dead for thousands of years could understand."[10] That may be true, but it *is* possible to know that the disciples *did not*

---

[5] J. Dwight Pentecost, *Things to Come* (Grand Rapids: Zondervan, 1958), 265.

[6] R. B. Thieme Jr., *The Divine Outline of History: Dispensations and the Church* (Houston, TX: R. B. Thieme Jr., Bible Ministries, 1989, 1999), 25.

[7] Ibid.

[8] Phillip D.R. Griffiths, *Covenant Theology: A Reformed Baptist Perspective* (Eugene OR: Wipf & Stock, 2016), 33.

[9] Ibid., 197.

[10] Corle, *What Salvation Is,* 253.

understand why Jesus was going to the cross, despite living alongside Him for three-and-a-half years (Mark 9:32). It is preposterous to teach that those who did *not* believe in the resurrection of Jesus were saved like we are today, when belief in His resurrection is a prerequisite for salvation today (Romans 10:9)! The disciples did *not* believe in the resurrection immediately after it took place (Mark 16:13–14), let alone during the earthly ministry of Christ. Read Matthew 16:21–22 to see how much Simon Peter was looking forward to the cross!

SLAIN FROM THE FOUNDATION

The idea that Old Testament saints were "saved by looking forward to the cross…in type"[11] is misleading. In fact, it is the same argument used by anti-dispensational reformed theologians to propagate their teaching of the Covenant of Grace.[12] Just because there are types of Christ's sacrifice and prophecies of His sacrifice in the Old Testament (like Isaiah 53 and Psalm 22), does not mean Jesus Christ's blood was appropriated to sinners before it was shed. Jesus Christ was in existence **"from everlasting, from the beginning, or ever the earth was"** (Proverbs 8:23), but Scripture never states that His blood was shed *before* the foundation of the world like Calvinists and revised dispensationalists teach. Revelation 13:8 does *not* say "the Lamb was slain from the foundation of the world." It says, **"the book of life of the Lamb slain from the foundation of the world."** The context, as well as

---

[11] Melton, "Understanding Dispensational Salvation."

[12] Daniel Hyde, "What is the Covenant of Grace," Ligonier Ministries, accessed August 13, 2019, http://www.ligonier.org/blog /what-covenant-grace/.

the object in the passage is **"the book of life,"** not **"the Lamb slain."** Revelation 17:8 clears up any misunderstanding when it states this truth again, this time omitting the phrase **"the Lamb slain."** And while His sacrifice might have been **"foreordained before the foundation of the world"** (1 Peter 1:20), Scripture is specific about *when* the atonement was made—in time:

> Nor yet that he should offer himself often, as the high priest entereth into the holy place every year with blood of others; For then must he often have suffered since the foundation of the world: but now once in the end of the world hath he appeared to put away sin by the sacrifice of himself. (Hebrews 9:25–26)

> But when the fulness of the time was come, God sent forth his Son, made of a woman, made under the law, To redeem them that were under the law, that we might receive the adoption of sons. (Galatians 4:4–5)

At first glance some KJO revised dispensationalists seem to be on the right road when they teach,

> it is quite obvious that those who died before the cross were not looking forward to the cross for salvation any more than these apostles were looking forward to it."[13]

They correctly say, "we must reject the old theory that men before the cross were saved because they looked forward to the cross."[14] But then they take a wrong turn at Calvin's crossroads by weaving

---

[13] Stauffer and Ray, *One Book Rightly Divided Prophetic Edition*, 339.

[14] Knox, *The Law and Rightly Dividing the Word Reconsidered*, 257.

the "unfolding theme of blood-bought redemption" throughout every dispensation because "it [redemption] was still there in the mind of God."[15]

In effect, this is what they are asserting: Since "God looked forward to the cross"[16] and knew "about the future redemptive work of the cross from the very beginning,"[17] this means,

> salvation before the cross was a matter of imputed righteousness, freely given to those who put their faith in the Lord and that such a gift was given without works.[18]

The Calvinistic undertones of KJO revised dispensationalists are hard to miss, especially when they emphasize, "a person is saved by faith alone in any dispensation" and, "there has only ever been one plan of salvation, and it was worked out and settled before the foundation of the world (1 Pet. 1:19–20; Rev. 13:8)."[19] According to this revised dispensational teaching, "Old Testament saints had the assurance that if they were gathered unto the fathers...they would one day be gathered unto Christ."[20] Their claim is that salvation in any age is "facilitated only through the perfect, spotless blood of Christ,"[21] even if the person did not actually put his faith in that precious blood! KJO revised dispensationalists cannot give *one Bible verse* from the Old Testament showing anyone putting

---

[15] Melton, "Understanding Dispensational Salvation."
[16] Knox, *The Law and Rightly Dividing the Word Reconsidered*, 254.
[17] Stauffer and Ray, *One Book Rightly Divided Prophetic Edition*, 667.
[18] Knox, *The Law and Rightly Dividing the Word Reconsidered*, 281.
[19] Tabb, *Dispensational Salvation*, 90.
[20] Stauffer and Ray, *One Book Rightly Divided Prophetic Edition*, 500.
[21] Ibid., 654.

faith in the Lord Jesus Christ for salvation. The implications of this *saved the same* scenario are absurd.

Eternal Security in Every Age?

The revised dispensationalists answer to the obvious faith-and-works salvation paradigm in other ages is far from satisfactory. As we have already seen, they see "the punishment threatened" in Ezekiel 18 to "refer only to physical death rather than to eternal death,"[22] even though the rational conclusion of spiritual death is implied by the use of the word **"soul."** Furthermore, the truth that spiritual circumcision is only applicable *after* the resurrection of Christ obliterates their position (John 7:38–39; Colossians 2:11–12).

Before a person is saved, his soul is stuck to his flesh. Consequently, every sin he commits in the flesh affects his soul. It is only after the resurrection of Jesus Christ that a believer has the promise of the sealing and permanent indwelling Holy Spirit (Ephesians 1:13, 4:30; 2 Corinthians 1:22). This means every Old Testament Jew under the Law had a dead spirit and was never born again, regardless of his "righteousness" or "wickedness," or whether he was considered "saved" or "lost." The word **"saved"** is not used exclusively for believers in the Church Age. Noah was **"saved"** (2 Peter 2:5), the Jews that came out of Egypt were **"saved"** (Jude 5), people were **"saved"** from their sins *and* physical maladies during the ministry of Christ (Luke 7:50, 18:42), and future **"nations"** will be **"saved"** (Revelation 21:24) after the

---

[22] *The Scofield Study Bible III*, 1063.

Millennium is over. No one could be **"born again"** (John 3) until *after* the resurrection of Christ, and the sealing work of the Holy Spirit which guarantees eternal security is *only applicable to Church Age saints!*

KJO revised dispensationalists think people during the earthly ministry of Christ were born again because of Jesus' conversation with Nicodemus.[23] They emphasize that "Jesus did not preach 'keep the Law and be born again', He called on men to believe on him,"[24] while leaving out the fact that Peter was not **"converted"** during that time (Luke 22:32) even though he did **"believe"** (John 6:69). Additionally, they fail to notice the ones **"who first trusted in Christ"** (Ephesians 1:12) were *not* "believers" who followed Christ prior to the resurrection. No "believer" who followed Jesus in His earthly ministry **"trusted in Christ"** in the same way we do today, and neither were they blessed with eternal security by being in the body of Christ like believers are today.

The honest student of the Bible will not overlook the purpose of John's gospel (John 20:31), nor *when* it was written. John wrote his books *after* Paul had written all his epistles. John had access to all of Paul's epistles containing the revealed truth of the mystery of the body of Christ, and was writing *after* salvation by grace through faith without works had been accepted by all the apostles (Acts 15:11).

If "a man who is sanctified by the blood of Christ NEVER loses that sanctification"[25] then no Old Testament saint ever lost his

---

[23] Stauffer and Ray, *One Book Rightly Divided Prophetic Edition*, 715.

[24] Knox, *The Law and Rightly Dividing the Word Reconsidered*, 68.

[25] Stauffer and Ray, *One Book Rightly Divided Prophetic Edition*, 221.

salvation, and no future Tribulation saint will ever be in danger of losing his salvation. This foolish teaching suggests a man like Saul (who lost the Holy Spirit—1 Samuel 16:14, 28:15–16) went to heaven (via. Abraham's bosom). The fact that an apparition, conjured up by necromancy, told Saul **"to morrow shalt thou and thy sons be with me"** (1 Samuel 28:19) does *not* "indicat[e] that Saul lost the Spirit but did not lose his salvation."[26] If necromancy was forbidden by God (Deuteronomy 18:10–11), why would God use it to communicate with Saul? Also, if salvation is the same in all ages, why could Old Testament saints lose the Holy Spirit when we can't in this age? Besides, even if the words of *Samuel* were true, they would have a broader application, because everyone before the cross went to the center of the earth at death (see Matthew 12:40 and Acts 2:27). Scripture refers to divisions in the heart of the earth as **"lower parts"** (Psalm 63:9; Isaiah 44:23; Ephesians 4:9), including both a **"place of torment"** (Luke 16:28), Abraham's bosom, and **"paradise"** (Luke 23:43). If Saul was "saved" why is he not mentioned in between Samuel and David in the heroes of the faith chapter (Hebrews 11)? Samson is mentioned, because, even though he lost the Spirit of God (Judges 16:20), he got it back after he prayed and was filled with strength (Judges 16:28).

These errors lead to the heresy of Lordship salvation and a denial of the biblical teaching of standing and state. And, to defend this position, revised dispensationalists must concede to the last point of Calvinism—the "p" in the "Tulip" acronym—"perseverance of the saints."

---

[26] Ibid., 239.

WORKS *BECAUSE OF* FAITH?

Once someone accepts the idea that salvation is the same in every age, it is easy for them to be contaminated by Calvinism. The naïve student assumes since we are **"justified by faith without the deeds of the law"** (Romans 3:28) *now,* all saints in every age were justified by faith and will be justified by faith in the future as well.

The problem is the occurrence of numerous verses that teach just the opposite, such as Romans 2:6–13? In Romans chapter two, the apostle Paul chronicled previous dispensations prior to Calvary when Jews followed the Law, and Gentiles followed their conscience. The Scripture says, **"the doers of the law shall be justified"** (Romans 2:13), not just those who "believed" or "had faith." And then there is the teaching of James, who taught, **"by works a man is justified, and not by faith only"** (James 2:24). At this point the student has a choice, as do you. You can either be honest and approach the Bible as a believer, laying aside any preconceived system that forces all verses to fit *your salvation*, or you can **"wrest…the…scriptures"** to fit your ideas (2 Peter 3:16). Once you dismiss the truth of dispensational salvation differences, then it really does not matter if the book of James is addressed to **"to the twelve tribes which are scattered abroad"** (James 1:1). Once you resolve that "the shed blood of Christ is the one constant throughout every period"[27] even though Jesus shed His blood *in time,* you are finished as far as being a Bible student—and that is exactly what KJO revised dispensationalist have done.

---

[27] Ibid., 794.

KJO revised dispensationalists adopt the Calvinist cliché' and theological idea that, "True faith is never alone. It always manifests itself in works."[28] This axiom has been repeated for years by hillbilly Baptist preachers who never studied the Bible, as well as pseudo–Independent Fundamental Baptist intellectuals who worship their own ministries. The verbiage, "perseverance and works are the *evidence* of salvation"[29] is practical Calvinism, plain and simple. Here's how it plays out: If someone does not have good works (like theirs!) and quits coming to church or tithing, the pious pastor says, "Well, they were never 'truly saved' to begin with." It is the old *profession without possession* line and is often put this way:

> Someone can claim to be saved and go through the outward motions of believing without truly being saved...[they] indicate by their actions that they were never truly saved.[30]

This is how they approach and mangle the book of James to fit doctrinal teachings for this age. They say, "Works do not save, but true salvation always produces good works."[31] The logical conclusion ends with a nice "p" on the end of the word "Tulip." *Perseverance of the saints* is the teaching that a *true* believer *will* persevere and live a life of good works *unto the end.* It's a good thing that John Mark did not die subsequently after he defected and

---

[28] R.C. Sproul, *What Is Reformed Theology* (Grand Rapids, MI: Baker Books, 1997, 2016), 83.

[29] David Cloud, *What About Ruckman* (Port Huron, MI: Way of Life Literature, 2012), 32.

[30] Stauffer and Ray, *One Book Rightly Divided Prophetic Edition,* 251.

[31] Ibid., 274.

left the mission field, or we never would have known he was *truly saved* (Acts 13:15).

TRIBULATION SALVATION

GOOD FOUNDATIONS

On a *recognized* scale, progressive revelation ended with Scofield and Larkin. The crescendo of great Bible teaching fell during the revised era where *scholars* replaced *students* and likewise rejected the purity of the Authorized Version. They could only take so much truth, and as far as premillennial dispensationalism was concerned, they never took it to the next level by **"rightly dividing"** (2 Timothy 2:15) soteriology, especially as it related to eschatology and the future Tribulation.

Dispensational premillennialism precisely and accurately defended the truth of the pre-Tribulational rapture of the church.[1] Classic dispensationalism reinforced the significant boundaries between the Church Age and the future Tribulation, noting that a

---

[1] Richard R. Reiter, "A History of the Development of the Rapture Positions," in *Three Views on the Rapture*, ed. Gleason L. Archer Jr. (Grand Rapids: Zondervan, 1996), 11–33.

different gospel would be preached after the Rapture. Haldeman correctly identified the gospel that will be preached to Jews after the rapture of the Church as the *gospel of the kingdom*.[2] Both Scofield and Larkin taught differences between the four gospels and Scofield outlined all four in *The Scofield Reference Bible* note on Revelation 14:6 where he defined each gospel. This note is changed in *The Scofield Study Bible III* to reinforce the revised position:

> the word 'gospel,' therefore, includes various aspects of the good news...[and] does not mean that there is more than one gospel of salvation. Grace is the basis for salvation in all dispensations.[3]

SHIFTING SAND

KJO revised dispensationalists likewise have rejected the truth of "a faith-and-works setup in the Tribulation (the last half of Daniel's Seventieth Week) which does not match the faith-and-grace setup found in the Church Age in the Body of Christ."[4] They, as many good Independent Baptists, believe there are no verses "in either Testament which teac[h] salvation can be lost,"[5] even though prophetic portions of the New Testament are replete with them (Matthew 10:22, 32–33, 19:29, 24:13–14; Hebrews 2:1, 3, 3:6, 14, 4:1, 9–11, 5:9, 6:4–12, 10:23–27, 12:14–15; James 2:14–26, 5:8–9,

---

[2] I. M. Haldeman, *Sermons on the Second Coming* (New York: Charles C. Cook, 1916–1917), 306–7.

[3] *The Scofield Study Bible III*, 1672.

[4] Peter S. Ruckman, "The Big Flap," *Bible Believers' Bulletin* 7 (November 1984): 1.

[5] Tabb, *Dispensational Salvation*, 74.

12; Revelation 1:3, 2:7, 11, 17, 26, 3:3, 5, 11–12, 21, 12:17, 14:12, 22:14, et al.).

Some KJO revised dispensational authors, to prove "Paul's intended audience" in Hebrews 6 was *only* Church Age believers say, "Paul did not write, '*For it is impossible for US…If WE shall fall away,*' etc."[6] in Hebrews chapter six while ignoring the personal pronouns **"us"** and **"we"** in Hebrews 4:1–14 and Hebrews 10:22–26. Their exegesis of Hebrews 10:26 removes **"we"** out of the passage altogether, stating, "the Jews in danger of the willful sin were Jews who knew that Jesus was the Christ."[7]

KJO revised dispensationalists follow in the steps of apostate revised dispensational Bible correctors like Dwight Pentecost, who taught, "Salvation in the Tribulation will certainly be on the faith principle."[8] Diverting from the plain truth of the verses, revised authors revert to the *physical life argument*, stressing "the difference between the earthly promises and eternal salvation"[9] while upholding eternal security for all Tribulation saints. According to their teaching, only "the lost" can take the mark of the beast.[10]

To skirt around the many verses teaching faith-and-works as a requirement for salvation in the Tribulation, KJO revised dispensationalists employ a couple of tactics. Some simply pretend these verses are not in the Bible. One author, in his 613-page book

---

[6] Stauffer and Ray, *One Book Rightly Divided Prophetic Edition,* 232–33.

[7] Ibid., 217.

[8] Pentecost, *Things to Come,* 269.

[9] James Knox, *The Book of Revelation* (DeLand FL: The BIBLE Baptist Church of DeLand, 1999), 475–476.

[10] Doug Stauffer, "The Tribulation Salvation Controversy", Sermon Audio, accessed July 10, 2019, https://media-cloud.sermonaudio.com/text/1319212404681.pdf.

on Revelation could not seem to locate Revelation 12:17, 14:12, and 22:14. He only commented on Revelation 12:17 by merely mentioning what "Larkin suggests"[11] about the groups being different. He skipped over Revelation 14:12 completely (page 480) as well as Revelation 22:14 (601–602). Another KJO revised dispensationalist wrote a book that supposedly covers "the passages from the book of Revelation used to teach a works salvation in the Tribulation period and the coming kingdom age"[12] while somehow neglecting to discuss Revelation 22:14 altogether.

Most KJO revised dispensationalists follow their predecessors like the editors of the *New Scofield Reference Bible,* or fundamentalists like Oliver B. Greene,[13] and M. R. DeHaan, who taught the passages (like Hebrews 6) referred to losing a "reward"[14] instead of losing salvation. They also insist Revelation 2:7 along with 2:11, 17, and 26 has "to do with rewards,"[15] and make the blunder of consigning parts of New Testament prophecy to the historical church in this age.[16] Passages in Hebrews, James, and Revelation that are prophetic *most certainly* "apply to Daniel's Seventieth Week," regardless of "the intended recipients of the epistle when it was written."[17] If the Bible only has application to the people in the days or years in which it was written, then most of it is entirely irrelevant and useless to us today! There are prophecies in the minor

---

[11] Knox, *The Book of Revelation,* 445.

[12] Tabb, *Dispensational Salvation,* 3.

[13] Oliver B. Greene, *Revelation* (Greenville: The Gospel Hour, 1963), 70.

[14] E. Schuyler English, ed., *The New Scofield Reference Bible* (New York: Oxford, 1967), 1315.

[15] Tabb, *Dispensational Salvation,* 81.

[16] Ibid.

[17] Stauffer and Ray, *One Book Rightly Divided Prophetic Edition,* 227.

prophets (Hosea—Malachi) still awaiting fulfillment. Similarly, there are portions of prophecy in the Gospels (Mathew 24 for instance), Paul's epistles (2 Thessalonians 2 for instance), and Hebrews—Revelation that are *not* Church Age doctrine because they are prophetic, dealing with salvation *after* the Rapture of the body of Christ.

When commenting on the few verses in Revelation that clearly prove faith-and-works (Revelation 12:17, 14:12), one reviser twisted the phrase **"testimony of Jesus"** to mean that the remnant has "the testimony that they 'keep the commandments of God.'"[18] That is *not* what the verse said at all. This same teacher used the example of a believer today getting baptized to prove his point:

> Those who keep the commandments of God are identified as the saints. This is similar to a Christian who follows the Lord in believer's baptism today. Getting baptized does not save but it surely identifies the believers and sometimes brings the persecution. Keeping the commandments in Daniel's Seventieth Week does not make someone a saint but it surely identifies the believers and will bring the persecution.[19]

This logic is Calvinistic at its core. The Calvinistic Reformation mantra from Luther (who was a Calvinist Augustinian monk before his conversion) was, "We are saved by faith alone, but the faith that saves is never alone."[20] KJO revised dispensationalists echo the

---

[18] Doug Stauffer, "Tribulation Salvation: Nothing but the Blood," Doug Stauffer Ministries, accessed July 10, 2019, https://www.dougstauffer.com/2019/04/tribulation-salvation-by-blood.html.

[19] Stauffer, "The Tribulation Salvation Controversy."

[20] Martin Luther, Azquotes.com, accessed November 30, 2023, https://www.azquotes.com/author/9142-Martin_Luther/tag/faith

same sentiment, avowing that "faith, real faith, includes works."[21] So, if you are *truly saved* or *really saved* then you will have good works in any dispensation. Therefore, according to them, the reason Tribulation saints keep the commandments is because they are saved to begin with. Pastor Donovan rightly debunks this thinking:

> So, we are to believe that under grace, with no pressure of life or death on him today, a saint of God can commit all kinds of sins and still be saved, but if one is saved during the tribulation period, he will not commit these sins and will endure to the end, waiting for the coming of Christ.[22]

OVERCOMING FOR SALVATION

The Bible is clear that *martyrdom* will be the only choice for many who wish to escape the judgment of the mark of the beast in the Tribulation:

> And they overcame him by the blood of the Lamb, and by the word of their testimony; and they loved not their lives unto the death. (Revelation 12:11)

Eventually, *most* overcomers will be martyred—**"beheaded for the witness of Jesus, and for the word of God"** (Revelation 20:4). Sharing the fate of the two witnesses (Moses and Elijah), the wording is that **"the beast…shall overcome them, and kill them"** (Revelation 11:7), but in reality, it will be the *martyrs* who **"overcame him** [the Antichrist] **by the blood of the Lamb, and**

---

[21] Melton, "Understanding Dispensational Salvation."
[22] Donovan, "A Marriage for His Son," 24.

by the word of their testimony; and they loved not their lives unto the death" (Revelation 12:11). Jesus foretold of those who would be willing to lose their lives for His sake (Matthew 10:39, 16:25; Mark 8:35; Luke 9:24, 17:33; John 12:25). KJO revised dispensationalists insist that "not loving their lives unto the death is the *fruit* of being an overcomer, not the *root* of overcoming."[23] This rhetoric is simply *refried Calvinism* that supports *Lordship salvation* and teaches "a true believer could never ultimately fail to overcome."[24] These circular statements are invented to sidestep clear warning passages throughout the transition books. These passages teach there will be *some* who **"were made partakers of the Holy Ghost"** who will **"fall away"** (Hebrews 6:5–6) and become irredeemable—falling **"back unto perdition"** (Hebrews 10:39).

Jesus, when prophesying of faithful servants in the Tribulation, said they **"shall be hated of all men for my name's sake."** Jesus then promised, **"but he that endureth to the end shall be saved"** (Matthew 10:22). Enduring to the end is *not* "dealing with *physical* salvation (or deliverance)."[25] After prophesying details of their persecution (Matthew 10:23), Jesus exhorts future Tribulation saints to **"fear not them which kill the body"** (Matthew 10:28), stressing the importance of *confessing* their faith (so they will not be denied before God—Matthew 10:32–33). Jesus also gives reassurance to those who lose their life for His sake:

---

[23] Stauffer, *Tribulation Salvation: Jesus Still Saves*, 47.

[24] MacArthur, *The Gospel According to Jesus*, 251.

[25] Stauffer and Ray, *One Book Rightly Divided: Prophetic Edition*, 52.

> He that findeth his life shall lose it: and he that loseth his life for my sake shall find it. (Matthew 10:39)

Additional corroboration of this view is found in Mark 8:35 where the phrase **"and the gospel's"** is added. This same **"gospel of the kingdom"** that was being preached during Christ's earthly ministry will also be **"preached in all the world for a witness unto all nations"** during the Tribulation (Matthew 24:14). This is why the disciples' commission passage of Matthew chapter ten matches the prophetic passage of Matthew chapter twenty-four. It also explains why there is a promise of protection from **"the second death"** for overcomers (Revelation 2:11). Overcomers will be protected from the *second* death (burning in **"the lake of fire"**—Revelation 20:14) even though most of them will experience the *first* death because they will confess Jesus and be martyred (Revelation 12:11, 20:4).

A Crystal-Clear Example

> Blessed are they that do his commandments, that they may have right to the tree of life, and may enter in through the gates into the city. (Revelation 22:14)

As clear as Revelation 22:14 is, you would think it would cause some Bible teachers to pause and consider its obvious implications—saints from the Tribulation will be given access to both **"the tree of life"** and **"the city"** New Jerusalem because of their obedience (works). Instead, apostates dismiss the AV because of the obvious truth it is proclaiming and accept the reading from corrupt manuscripts, like found in the Revised Version's (RV) rendering: "Blessed are they that wash their robes, that they may have the right *to come* to the tree of life, and may enter in by the gates into the city." Darby called the RV's translation of Revelation 22:14 "the true reading"[26] and Ironside said it was "in accordance with the best manuscripts"[27] which is simply not the case! This defective reading, "wash their robes" is also found in most modern versions and is based on the corrupt Siniaticus and Alexandrinus manuscripts which both contain the Apocrypha! William Pettingill called this perversion of the truth a "very important correction,"[28] but there is nothing in the verse to be "corrected." The King James reading is defended by the majority of extant manuscripts, the Harclean Syriac, the Bohairic (a Coptic version), and it was quoted by the church father Tertullian—proving it existed in AD 220 (*prior to the inception of Siniaticus and Alexandrinus*).[29] Gaebelein expounded on the reason they all rejected this text by saying, "the Authorized Version here is faulty...[because] eternal life and eternal glory cannot be obtained by keeping commandments."[30]

The problem was not a misunderstanding of what the AV was saying. The problem was actually believing the text. Jack Van Impe did not believe it,[31] John R. Rice called it a "mistranslation"[32]

---

[26] John Nelson Darby, *Synopsis of the Books of the Bible,* vol. 5, *Colossians—The Revelation* (London: G. Morrish, n.d.) 565.

[27] H. A. Ironside, *Lectures on the book of Revelation* (Neptune, NJ: Loizeaux Brothers, 1920), 364.

[28] William L. Pettingill, *Simple Studies in Revelation* (Harrisburg: Fred Kelker, 1906), 132.

[29] Eberhard Nestle et al., eds. *Novum Testamentum Graece,* 27th rev. ed. (Stuttgart Germany: Deutsche Bibelgesellschaft, 1993), 680.

[30] Arno C. Gaebelein, *The Revelation: An Analysis and Exposition of the Last Book of the Bible* (New York: Our Hope, 1915), 173.

[31] Jack Van Impe, *Revelation Revealed* (Royal Oak, MI: Jack Van Impe Ministries, 1982), 252.

[32] Herbert F. Evans, *Dear Dr. John: Where is my Bible?* (Harlingen, TX: Wonderful Word Publishers, 1976), 3–4.

because he did not believe it. Oliver B. Greene did not believe it,[33] and neither did Henry Morris, who stated, "it is surely true that any person who is genuinely saved will love His commandments and seek to keep them."[34]

KJO revised dispensationalists side with those who find fault with the Authorized Version. But instead of faulting the AV text as being incorrect, they just deny what everyone *knows* the verse is saying. One KJO revised dispensationalist said, "The doing of God's commandments does not convey salvation...This may refer to those who in his life have turned to Christ..."[35] Another KJO revised dispensationalist bypassed the clear teaching of those verses much like Morris. He said tribulation saints "are simply saved, obedient, saints. Is that not our case today? Are we who are saved not also obedient to the Lord?"[36] Professing to be dispensationalists, these men are actually riding down a reformed theology roller coaster that compliments the false teaching of Lordship salvation. So, according to them, any Tribulation saint will overcome and endure till the end; if he does not endure, he never was saved to begin with.

The truth of the matter is that keeping and doing God's commandments during the Tribulation grants two things for Tribulation saints: partaking of the tree of life (which gives eternal life—Genesis 3:22) and entering New Jerusalem. The believer in the Church Age is granted eternal life by *faith*, through the ear

---

[33] Greene, *Revelation*, 535.

[34] Henry Morris, ed., *The Defenders Study Bible* (Grand Rapids: Word, 1995), 1468.

[35] David H. Sorenson, *Understanding the Bible: Hebrews through Revelation* (Duluth: Northstar Ministries, 2008), 566–567.

[36] Tabb, *Dispensational Salvation*, 83.

canal, not orally through the digestive system! Also, we are not waiting to go through the gate, we *are part of the gate!*

> ...Come hither, I will shew thee the bride, the Lamb's wife...shewed me that great city, the holy Jerusalem, descending out of heaven from God. (Revelation 21:9–10)

PRE-TRIBULATION RAPTURE A BIG DEAL?

If salvation is the same during the Tribulation as it is during the Church Age; if Tribulation saints are sealed with the Holy Spirit, placed in the body of Christ, and guaranteed eternal security—then why should we "refute all objections raised against" the pre-Tribulation Rapture of the church?[37] *What is the big fuss* over this doctrine if there are no repercussions for the believer going through the Tribulation? If we are *not* raptured before the Tribulation, we would not have anything to worry about if salvation is the same in the Tribulation.

On the other hand, *if* the church is *not* raptured before the Tribulation, and taking the mark of the beast *does* send a person to hell (Revelation 14:11), then the Rapture *must precede* the Tribulation. If the warnings about losing salvation during the Tribulation *are* true—going through the Tribulation would pose more problems than mere physical persecution for the Christian. It would mean God, who has promised eternal salvation for all believers in this age, would be a liar. Thank God, we know that cannot happen. We might have some hard times in front of us, but the possibility

---

[37] James W. Knox, "Introduction" in *That Blessed Hope: Teaching and Defending the Doctrine of the Rapture of the Church,* James W. Knox et. al. (DeLand, FL: The BIBLE Baptist Church, 2016), 9.

of damnation is *not* in our future—seeing Jesus Christ is our future (Philippians 3:20; 1 Thessalonians 5:9).

SALVATION DIFFERENCES

For Church Age saints, the blood of Jesus Christ is applied the moment of repentance and faith in Christ (Romans 5:9; Ephesians 1:7, 2:13; Colossians 1:14). At that moment of belief, the Holy Spirit permanently seals the believer (Ephesians 1:13) through a spiritual **"operation of God"** called **"the circumcision of Christ"** (Colossians 2:11–12). Simultaneously, the believer is placed in the body of Christ and becomes a part of His bride—the church (Romans 12:5; 1 Corinthians 15:22; Ephesians 1:22–23).

Tribulation saints are either Jews or Gentiles. They are *not* a part of the church and are therefore *not* in the body of Christ and *cannot* be sealed with the Holy Spirit and have eternal security. This is why *every* verse dealing with Tribulation salvation gives the contingency of losing salvation. The nation of Israel is the bride of Jehovah (Hosea 2:2) that has been *divorced* from God for over two thousand years. At the Rapture, the predominantly *Gentile* bride (Romans 11:11–13) will be taken up to marry her Bridegroom—the Lord Jesus Christ (Revelation 19:7–9). The set-aside Jewish bride will be allured by God (Hosea 2:14). This is pictured in the book of Esther when Vashti, the Gentile bride, is replaced with the Jewish bride, Esther.

The group that **"washed their robes"** are said to have come **"out of great tribulation"** (Revelation 7:14). The Church Age saint will not go in or come out of the Tribulation; and neither will he wash his robe, because *he himself has been washed* by the blood of Jesus (1 Corinthians 6:11; 1 Peter 1:18–19; 1 John 1:7; Revelation 1:5). There are two "washings" mentioned in connection with the Church Age saint (Ephesians 5:26; Titus 3:5), and neither is done by the saint—they are done by the Saviour! Furthermore, if our robes were washed, they would not be washed by us, for that would be works and faith, as opposed to **"faith only"** (James 2:24). Also, a robe is an outer garment and is different from the inner garments (2 Corinthians 5:2–4) which are connected to our works, **"for the fine linen is the righteousness of saints"** (Revelation 19:8).

Church Age doctrine will be *non-applicable* during the last half of Daniel's seventieth week, **"the time of Jacob's trouble"** (Jeremiah 30:7). Since the Tribulation and the Millennium fall under the *New Testament*, the blood of that Testament will be applied *corporately* to the nation of Israel when they are converted at the second advent. This will initiate the *New Covenant*:

> Repent ye therefore, and be converted, that your sins may be blotted out, when the times of refreshing shall come from the presence of the Lord. (Acts 3:19)

> And so all Israel shall be saved: as it is written, There shall come out of Sion the Deliverer, and shall turn away ungodliness from Jacob: For this *is* my covenant unto them, when I shall take away their sins. (Romans 11:26–27)

> Behold, the days come, saith the LORD, that I will make a new covenant with the house of Israel, and with the house of Judah: Not according to the covenant that I made with their fathers in the day *that* I took them by the hand to bring them out of the land of Egypt; which my covenant they brake, although I was an husband unto them, saith

the LORD: But this *shall be* the covenant that I will make with the house of Israel; After those days, saith the LORD, I will put my law in their inward parts, and write it in their hearts; and will be their God, and they shall be my people. And they shall teach no more every man his neighbour, and every man his brother, saying, Know the LORD: for they shall all know me, from the least of them unto the greatest of them, saith the LORD: for I will forgive their iniquity, and I will remember their sin no more. (Jeremiah 31:31–34)

In those days, and in that time, saith the LORD, the iniquity of Israel shall be sought for, and *there shall be* none; and the sins of Judah, and they shall not be found: for I will pardon them whom I reserve. (Jeremiah 50:20)

I have blotted out, as a thick cloud, thy transgressions, and, as a cloud, thy sins: return unto me; for I have redeemed thee. (Isaiah 44:22)

For the Tribulation saints, salvation will come in the future (James 1:21) when they are delivered at the second advent, raptured, or martyred for their testimony (Romans 11:26–27; Revelation 14:1, 20:4). *Instant conversion* (like today in the Church Age), where a person becomes a member of God's family by belief (Galatians 3:26), is foreign under the Law *and* during the Tribulation. Jews in the Old Testament were *born* **"the people of God"** (Judges 20:2; 2 Samuel 14:13; Hebrews 4:9), and Jews in the Tribulation are considered God's *servants* even if they are wicked servants who lose their salvation (Matthew 24:48–51). Some KJO revised dispensational authors make these servants "Jews who fail to trust in the Lord,"[38] even though *both* the wicked and faithful

---

[38] Douglas D. Stauffer and Andrew B. Ray, *When the End Begins: Refuting a Rapture in Matthew 24–25* (Knoxville, TN: McCowen Mills Publishers & LTB Publications, 2017), 177.

servants are called **"his own servants"** (Matthew 25:14) before they are judged by their *works*.

No Old Testament saint or Tribulation saint is *born again* like a Church Age saint (2 Corinthians 5:17). The *new birth* for Israel is a *national birth* not an individual birth, and it occurs at the second advent (Isaiah 49:20–22, 66:8; Micah 5:3; Revelation 12:2, etc.). The Jewish *body* of saints during the Tribulation may be **"in the Lord"** (Revelation 14:13), but they are *not* in **"the body of Christ"** (1 Corinthians 12:27). Believers in the body of Christ are not *merely* **"partakers of Christ"** (Hebrews 3:14) like Tribulation saints; they are **"members of Christ"** (1 Corinthians 6:15). Being a *partaker* of Christ is conditional. See **"if"** (Hebrews 3:14) and **"if they shall fall away"** (Hebrews 6:6). Believers in the Church Age are *not* **"partakers of the Holy Ghost"** (Hebrews 6:4); we are **"joined unto the Lord"** and are therefore **"one spirit"** (1 Corinthians 6:17). Tribulation saints will be saved by faith and works because, if they *backslide* and take the mark of the beast, they will lose that part of Christ they were *partaking of* and go to hell (Hebrews 6:1–8; Revelation 14:11). These truths explain the verses dealing with salvation during the Tribulation where it is obvious salvation can be lost.

THE RIGHT POSITION

The Bible-believing dispensational approach explains and answers what the revised position cannot. It also retains the integrity of the biblical divisions and distinctions between Israel and the body of Christ. If salvation is the same in the Tribulation as it is in the Church Age, then Tribulation saints are indwelt and sealed by the

Holy Ghost (Ephesians 1:13, 4:30) and also **"joined unto the Lord"** (1 Corinthians 6:16). Tribulation saints would then be *in the body of Christ*. How can Tribulation saints be in the body of Christ, when His body has been raptured and taken to heaven for the marriage of the Lamb?

The greatest proof for the pre-tribulation rapture of the Church is not ecclesiological or eschatological; it is soteriological. In other words, the Church has to be removed from the earth prior to the Rapture in order to escape **"the wrath to come"** (1 Thessalonians 1:10) and remain eternally secure. There is no *eternal security* during the Tribulation (except for the 144,000 witnesses).

There are different gospels being preached during the Tribulation other than **"the gospel of the grace of God"** (Acts 20:24) that is preached now in the Church Age (Matthew 24:14; Revelation 14:6). There is a distinction between Jews and Gentiles during the Tribulation that is not made now during the Church Age (Galatians 3:28; Revelation 7 and 14). Disobedient **"servants"** can lose their salvation during the Tribulation, while they *cannot* during the Church Age (Matthew 24:45–51; Romans 6:16).

Truth Misapplied

Right verse Wrong Dispensation

Over and over, KJO revised dispensationalists misapply truths for the Church Age into other dispensations. They use verses like Galatians 3:11 (**"But that no man is justified by the law in the sight of God, it is evident: for, The just shall live by faith."**) to prove that "it was never God's intent that one should seek to gain eternal life through the keeping of commandments,"[1] even though Galatians 3:11 is in the present tense, dealing with justification by faith in the Church Age. Romans 2:6–13 shows that prior to Calvary, if Jews or Gentiles wanted **"immortality"** and **"eternal life,"** they had to be **"doers of the law."** And while Galatians 3:21 is absolutely true (**"...for if there had been a law given which**

---

[1] Knox, *The Law and Rightly Dividing the Word Reconsidered,* 63.

could have given life, verily righteousness should have been by the law"), the rest of the Bible is true as well.

The confusion from revised dispensationalists comes from a few basic errors. First, is the acceptance (consciously or ignorantly) of the Calvinistic notion of God's *eternal decrees*. One KJO revised dispensationalist used John 14:6 and sermonized,

> Jesus did not say, "*Now I am the life.*" He said, "*I AM THE LIFE!*" He did not say, "*From now forward, I am the way.*" He said, "*I AM THE WAY!*"[2]

This type of Bible exposition foregoes the fact of progressive revelation, and is *non*-dispensational at its foundation. Jesus is **"the way"** (John 14:6), and men **"must be born again"** (John 3:7), but prior to Calvary no one, not even Nicodemus, could have been **"born of the Spirit"** (John 3:6) because **"the Holy Ghost was not yet given, because that Jesus was not yet glorified"** (John 7:39). Yes, the disciples **"believed"** (John 16:27), but they did not believe the resurrection at first (Mark 16:13–14), until He physically appeared unto them.

Second, the error is made by taking two types of our salvation to the extreme (Abraham and David). Abraham is a type of our salvation in the sense that he was given righteousness by God, not by believing in Christ's shed blood for his atonement, but by believing God would give him thousands of descendants (Genesis 15:5). David is a type of our salvation in the sense that God did not impute sin to him that he deserved (Romans 4:6–8). Paul could just

---

[2] James W. Knox, "The Church's One Foundation" in *One Book Rightly Divided Prophetic Edition,* Stauffer and Ray, 610.

as easily used Phinehas as an example of someone who had righteousness **"counted unto him"** (Psalm 106:31). And Phinehas no more believed on Jesus Christ for salvation than Abraham or David. He was given righteousness for stabbing and killing two fornicators (Numbers 25:7–8).

KJO revised dispensationalists assume the gospel of the death, burial, and resurrection of Christ was preached to Abraham because of Galatians 3:8.[3] But **"the gospel"** that was preached to Abraham is actually stated in the verse as, **"In thee shall all nations be blessed."** Types are just that—types. Abraham had faith in God's word, and he was given righteousness for believing God. It's that simple. Granted, "there is significance to the little phrase in Genesis 22:8, 'provide Himself a Lamb,'"[4] but that does not prove "salvation has always been by grace through faith in the shed blood of Jesus Christ."[5] Later in the same passage, Paul stated that **"the faith"** employed now, during the Church Age, is *after* the Law:

> But before faith came, we were kept under the law, shut up unto the faith which should **afterwards be revealed**. (Galatians 3:23)

Some KJO revised dispensationalists have the ridiculous idea that "David under law is shown to have been saved exactly the same way in which Abraham was."[6] Neither Abraham nor David were born again. David was worried about losing the Holy Spirit (Psalm 51:11). And Abraham might have been given imputed right-

---

[3] Ibid., 275.
[4] Corle, What *Salvation Is,* 250.
[5] Ibid., 253.
[6] Tabb, *Dispensational Salvation,* 6.

eousness by faith, but he was **"justified by works"** (James 2:21) so he could be a *dual type.* Note Pastor Donovan's comment:

> Paul uses Abraham as a picture of the "father" of those of faith for the Church Age in Romans and Galatians, while James uses Abraham as the literal physical **"father"** (James 2:21) of **"the twelve tribes which are scattered abroad"** (James 1:1) and the two examples are NOT the same.[7]

The change of salvation conditions in the different dispensations are apparent to *honest* Bible students willing to set aside their theological biases. An Old Testament saint's personal righteousness during the dispensation of the Law (see Deuteronomy 6:25, 24:13; 1 Samuel 26:23; 2 Samuel 22:21; 1 Kings 8:32; 2 Chronicles 6:23; Psalm 106:30–31), is *different* than a New Testament Christian's imputed righteousness received by faith (Romans 3:25–26). The **"righteousness"** spoken of in Galatians is not the personal righteousness by works of Old Testament saints. The **"righteousness of God without the law is manifested"** (Romans 3:21) now, *after* Calvary, not before! Old Testament saints could not have the righteousness of God because **"the righteousness of God…is by faith of Jesus Christ"** (Romans 3:22), and Jesus Christ had not come, bled, died, and been resurrected yet!

Dr. Ruckman clarified these points many times. He noted there is a reason "Paul omitted **'his'** from **'his faith'** (Hab. 2:4)" and that "it was no longer **'his'** it was God's"[8] (based on Ephesians 2:8–9). There is a reason Old Testament saints could not go directly to

---

[7] Donovan, "One Book Wrongly Divided…Twice," 15.

[8] Peter S. Ruckman, *The Death of Biblical Doctrine* (Pensacola: BB Bookstore, 2007), 31–32.

heaven at death—their sins were not cleared, and they were not redeemed (Exodus 34:7; Hebrews 10:4). And, while **"the prophets and Moses"** foretold of the death, burial, and resurrection of Christ (Acts 26:22–23), they only bore witness of **"him"** (Acts 10:43), not the change in dispensational salvation. For that **"gospel of the grace of God"** (Acts 20:24) dealt with a **"salvation the prophets have inquired and searched diligently."** They did not understand and believe by looking forward to it, rather, they prophesied about it, because it was a **"grace that should come,"** not one they were already experiencing:

> Of which salvation the prophets have inquired and searched diligently, who prophesied of the grace that should come unto you. (1 Peter 1:10)

Conclusion

"Charity before the church" (3 John 6)

In conclusion, I would like to be a bit more charitable to those brethren who are indeed King James Bible believers but are espousing the revised or classical dispensational position.

I am aware some of these men have made accusations against us—that we are "not Bible believers" because we "remain blinded to the truth;"[1] that we "got it all wrong" and are teaching "heresy;"[2] that we are not "respectable Bible teachers" because we "throw out all semblance of sanity" and "civility;"[3] that our "viewpoint…is the pinnacle of hypocrisy;"[4] that we "have neglected elements of the truth," causing us to be "careless" and "private interpret[ers];"[5] and

---

[1] Stauffer and Ray, *One Book Rightly Divided Prophetic Edition,* 201.
[2] Ibid., 488.
[3] Ibid., 490.
[4] Ibid., 504.
[5] Ibid., 516.

that we follow a "man-made philosophy"[6] that "is tenaciously held by a fringe group within fundamental Christianity."[7]

But I know many of these men are good men who love the Lord. It is my prayer that these men would be *honest with themselves* in front of the Book they are called to preach and rightly divide. May they be concerned what the Scriptures *say* not merely what they were taught. May their love for the *truth* outweigh their fear of ridicule and intimidation from the brethren.

---

[6] Ibid., 227.
[7] Knox, *The Law and Rightly Dividing the Word Reconsidered,* 257.

BIBLIOGRAPHY

Bateman IV, Herbert W. "Dispensationalism Yesterday and Today." In *Three Central Issues in Contemporary Dispensationalism,* edited by Herbert W. Bateman IV, 21–60. Grand Rapids: Kregel, 1999.

Bullinger, E. W. *The Companion Bible.* Grand Rapids: Kregel, 1990.

Campbell, Gordon. *Bible: The Story of the King James Version 1611–2011.* New York: Oxford University Press, 2010.

Chafer, Lewis Sperry. *Grace.* Philadelphia: The Sunday School Times, 1922.

———. *Systematic Theology.* Vol. 7, *Doctrinal Summarization.* Grand Rapids: Kregel, 1976.

Chappell, Paul. *Galatians: No Turning Back.* Lancaster, CA: Striving Together Publications, 2013.

Cloud, David. *What About Ruckman.* Port Huron, MI: Way of Life Literature, 2012.

Corle, Dennis. *What Salvation Is.* Claysburg, PA: Revival Fires! Publishing, 2015.

Cummings, Calvin Knox. "The Covenant of Grace." The Orthodox Presbyterian Church. Accessed August 13, 2019. http://www.opc.org/cce/covenant.html.

Darby, John Nelson. *Synopsis of the Books of the Bible.* Vol. 5, *Colossians — Revelation.* London: G. Morrish, n.d.

Dean Jr., Robert. "Essentials of Dispensational Theology." Dean Bible Ministries. Accessed August 13, 2019. https://www.deanbibleministries.org/file-downloads/preview?path=Doctrines%252FEssentials_of_Dispensational_Theology.pdf.

Donovan, Brian. "A Marriage for His Son." *Bible Believers' Bulletin* 41 (September 2017): 23–27.

———. "One Book Wrongly Divided…Twice." *Bible Believers' Bulletin* 43 (June 2016): 1, 8–16.

English, E. Schuyler, ed. *The New Scofield Reference Bible.* New York: Oxford, 1967.

Evans, Herbert F. *Dear Dr. John: Where is my Bible?* Harlingen, TX: Wonderful Word Publishers, 1976.

Gaebelein, Arno C. *The Revelation: An Analysis and Exposition of the Last Book of the Bible.* New York: Our Hope, 1915.

Geisler, Norman L. *Systematic Theology.* Vol. 4, *The Bible.* Bloomington, MN: Bethany House, 2005.

Gerstner, John H. *Wrongly Dividing the Word of Truth.* Morgan, PA: Soli Deo Gloria Publications, 2000.

BIBLIOGRAPHY

Greene, Oliver B. *Revelation.* Greenville, SC: The Gospel Hour, 1963.

Griffiths, Phillip D.R. *Covenant Theology: A Reformed Baptist Perspective.* Eugene OR: Wipf & Stock, 2016.

Haldeman, I.M. *Friday Night Papers, the Second Coming, and other Expositions.* New York: Theo. Audel & Company, 1901.

———. *Sermons on the Second Coming.* New York: Charles C. Cook, 1916–1917.

Hyde, Daniel. "What is the Covenant of Grace." Ligonier Ministries. Accessed August 13, 2019. http://www.ligonier.org/blog/what-covenant-grace/.

Ironside, H.A. *Lectures on the book of Revelation.* Neptune, NJ: Loizeaux Brothers, 1920.

Knox, James W. "The Church's One Foundation." In *One Book Rightly Divided Prophetic Edition,* Douglas D. Stauffer and Andrew B. Ray. Knoxville, TN: McCowen Mills Publishers & LTB Publications, 2018.

———. *The Law and Rightly Dividing the Word Reconsidered.* DeLand, FL: The Bible Baptist Church, 2009.

———. *The Book of Revelation.* DeLand FL: The Bible Baptist Church of DeLand, 1999.

———. *By Definition: A Readers Guide to the King James Bible.* DeLand, FL: The Bible Baptist Church of DeLand, 1996, 2013.

Kreider, Glenn R. "What is Dispensationalism." In *Dispensationalism and the History of Redemption,* eds. D.Jeffrey Bingham and Glenn R. Kreider, 15–46. Chicago: Moody, 2015.

Larkin, Clarence. *Rightly Dividing the Word.* Glenside, PA: Rev. Clarence Larkin Est., 1920.

Logan, Brent. "Arguments Against that Blessed Hope." In *That Blessed Hope: Teaching and Defending the Doctrine of the Rapture of the* Church, edited by James W. Knox, 245–62. DeLand, FL: The Bible Baptist Church, 2016.

Luther, Martin. Azquotes.com. Accessed November 30, 2023. https://www.azquotes.com/author/9142-Martin_Luther/tag/faith

MacArthur Jr., John. *The Gospel According to Jesus: What Is Authentic Faith?* Rev. ed. Grand Rapids: Zondervan, 2008.

Mangum, Todd R., and Mark S. Sweetnam. *The Scofield Bible.* Colorado Springs: Paternoster, 2009.

Marsden, George M. *Fundamentalism and American Culture.* New York: Oxford, 2006.

Mason Jr., Clarence E. *Dispensationalism Made Simple.* Glenside, PA: Self-Published, 1976.

Melton, James. "Understanding Dispensational Salvation." Bible Baptist Publications. Accessed August 7, 2019. https://www.biblebaptistpublications.org/dispensationalsalvation.html.

Milligan, Robert. *An Exposition and Defense of the Scheme of Redemption,* 3rd Rev. ed. Cincinnati: R.W. Carroll & Co., 1869.

Morris, Henry. ed. *The Defenders Study Bible.* Grand Rapids: Word, 1995.

Morris, James C. *Ancient Dispensational Truth: Refuting the Myth that Dispensationalism is New.* Taos, NM: Dispensational Publishing House, Inc., 2018.

Nestle, Eberhard and Erwin, Barbara and Kurt Aland, Johannes Karavidopoulos, Carlo Martini, and Bruce Metzger, eds. *Novum Testamentum Graece,* 27th rev. ed. Stuttgart Germany: Deutsche Bibelgesellschaft, 1993.

BIBLIOGRAPHY

Oats, Larry R. "Salvation in Dispensationalism." *Frontline Magazine* 20, no. 4 (July/August 2010): 10–12, https://fbfi.org/wp-content/uploads/2017/01/2010.08.FrontLine.pdf.

PCA Historical Center. "1944 PCUS Report on Dispensationalism." Accessed August 13, 2019. http://www.pcahistory.org/documents/pcus1944.html.

Pentecost, J. Dwight. *Things to Come: A Study in Biblical Eschatology.* Grand Rapids: Zondervan, 1958.

Pettingill, William L. *Simple Studies in Revelation.* Harrisburg, PA: Fred Kelker, 1906.

Reese, Ed. *Reese Chronological Encyclopedia of Christian Biographies.* Chattanooga: AMG, 2007.

Reiter, Richard R. "A History of the Development of the Rapture Positions." In *Three Views on the Rapture*, edited by Gleason L. Archer Jr., 9–44. Grand Rapids: Zondervan, 1996.

Ruckman, Peter S. *How to Teach Dispensational Truth.* Pensacola: Bible Believers Press, 1992.

———. "The Big Flap." *Bible Believers' Bulletin* 7 (November 1984): 1–8.

———. *The Death of Biblical Doctrine.* Pensacola: BB Bookstore, 2007.

———. *The Ruckman Reference Bible.* Pensacola: Bible Baptist Bookstore, 2009.

Ryrie, Charles C. *Dispensationalism.* Rev. ed. Chicago: Moody Press, 1995.

Scofield, C. I. ed., *Scofield Reference Bible.* New York: Oxford University Press, 1909.

Scofield, C. I., E. Schuyler English, and Doris W. Rikkers, eds. *The Scofield Study Bible III.* New York: Oxford, 2003.

Sorenson, David H. *Understanding the Bible: Hebrews through Revelation.* Duluth, MN: Northstar Ministries, 2008.

Sproul, R.C. *What Is Reformed Theology.* Grand Rapids, MI: Baker Books, 1997, 2016.

Stauffer Douglas D., and Andrew B. Ray. *One Book Rightly Divided: Prophetic Edition.* Knoxville, TN: McCowen Mills Publishers & LTB Publications, 2018.

———. *When the End Begins: Refuting a Rapture in Matthew 24–25.* Knoxville, TN: McCowen Mills Publishers & LTB Publications, 2017.

Stauffer, Douglas D. *One Book Rightly Divided Expanded Edition.* Millbrook, AL: McCowen Mills Publishers, 1999, 2000, 2006.

———. *One Book Rightly Divided Second Edition.* Millbrook, AL: McCowen Mills Publishers, 1999, 2000).

———. "The Tribulation Salvation Controversy." Sermon Audio. Accessed July 10, 2019. https://mediacloud.sermonaudio.com/text/1319212404681.pdf.

———. *Tribulation Salvation: Jesus Still Saves.* Niceville, FL: McCowen Mills Publishers, 2020.

———. "Tribulation Salvation: Nothing but the Blood." Doug Stauffer Ministries. Accessed July 10, 2019. http://www.dougstauffer.com/2019/04/tribulation-salvation-by-blood.html.

Tabb, M.H. *Dispensational Salvation.* Ft. Walton Beach, FL: Foundation Ministries, 1991.

———. *The Gap Theory.* Fort Walton Beach, FL: Foundation Ministries, 1993.

Thieme Jr., R. B. *The Divine Outline of History: Dispensations and the Church.* Houston, TX: R. B. Thieme Jr., Bible Ministries, 1989, 1999.

Van Impe, Jack. *Revelation Revealed.* Royal Oak, MI: Jack Van Impe Ministries, 1982.

Watson, William C. *Dispensationalism before Darby.* Silverton, OR: Lampion Press, 2015.

Wilkinson, Paul Richard. *For Zion's Sake.* Eugene: Wipf & Stock, 2007.

Witheringon III, Ben. *The Problem with Evangelical Theology: Testing the Exegetical Foundations of Calvinism, Dispensationalism, and Wesleyanism.* Waco: Baylor University Press, 2005.

SCRIPTURE INDEX

GENESIS

Genesis 3:15, 21
Genesis 3:22, 40
Genesis 15:5, 48
Genesis 22:8, 49

EXODUS

Exodus 20:6, 15
Exodus 24:7, 13
Exodus 34:7, 51

NUMBERS

Numbers 25:7–8, 49
Numbers 27:20, 13

DEUTERONOMY

Deuteronomy 6:25, 50
Deuteronomy 7:9, 15
Deuteronomy 8:20, 13
Deuteronomy 18:10–11, 27
Deuteronomy 24:13, 50
Deuteronomy 25:1, 13

JOSHUA

Joshua 22:2, 15

JUDGES

Judges 2:17, 15
Judges 16:20, 27
Judges 16:28, 27
Judges 20:2, 44

1 SAMUEL

1 Samuel 16:14, 27
1 Samuel 26:23, 50
1 Samuel 28:15–16, 27
1 Samuel 28:19, 27

2 SAMUEL

2 Samuel 22:21, 50
2 Samuel 14:13, 44

1 KINGS

1 Kings 3:3, 15
1 Kings 8:32, 50
1 Kings 11:34, 15

2 KINGS

2 Kings 18:6, 15

2 CHRONICLES

2 Chron. 6:23, 9, 50
2 Chron. 34:2, 15

PSALMS

Psalm 7:8, 18
Psalm 9:17, 17
Psalm 22, 22
Psalm 25:21, 18
Psalm 26:11, 18

Psalm 41:12, 18
Psalm 51:11, 49
Psalm 63:9, 27
Psalm 106:30–31, 49, 50
Psalm 119:99, 1

PROVERBS
Proverbs 8:23, 22
Proverbs 19:16, 16
Proverbs 24:12, 13

ISAIAH
Isaiah 1:19, 13
Isaiah 24:24, 13
Isaiah 44:22, 44
Isaiah 44:23, 27
Isaiah 49:20–22, 45
Isaiah 53, 22
Isaiah 66:8, 45

JEREMIAH
Jeremiah 30:7, 43
Jeremiah 31:31–34, 43, 44
Jeremiah 50:20, 44

EZEKIEL
Ezekiel 18, 16, 25
Ezekiel 18:10–11, 17
Ezekiel 18:14, 17
Ezekiel 18:20, 17
Ezekiel 18:21, 17
Ezekiel 18:23, 17
Ezekiel 18:24, 17
Ezekiel 18:27, 13
Ezekiel 43:19, 20

HOSEA
Hosea 2:2, 42
Hosea 2:14, 42

MICAH
Micah 5:3, 45

HABAKKUK

Habakkuk 2:4, 50

MATTHEW

Matthew 10:22, 32, 37
Matthew 10:23, 37

Matthew 10:28, 37
Matthew 10:32–33, 32, 37
Matthew 10:39, 37, 38
Matthew 12:40, 27
Matthew 16:21–22, 22
Matthew 16:25, 37
Matthew 19:29, 32
Matthew 24, 35
Matthew 24:13–14, 32
Matthew 24:14, 38, 46
Matthew 24:45–51, 46
Matthew 24:48–51, 44
Matthew 25:14, 45

MARK
Mark 8:35, 37, 38
Mark 9:32, 22
Mark 16:13–14, 22, 48

LUKE
Luke 7:50, 25
Luke 9:24, 37
Luke 16:22, 17
Luke 16:28, 27
Luke 17:33, 37
Luke 18:42, 25
Luke 22:32, 26
Luke 23:43, 27
Luke 24:49, 17

JOHN

John 1:17, 5, 10
John 3, 26
John 3:6, 48
John 3:7, 48
John 6:69, 26
John 7:38–39, 17, 25
John 7:39, 48
John 8:24, 16
John 12:25, 37
John 14:6, 48
John 16:27, 48
John 20:31, 26

ACTS

Acts 2:27, 27
Acts 2:38, 17
Acts 3:19, 43
Acts 5:14, 13

Acts 10:43, 51
Acts 10:45, 17
Acts 11:17, 17
Acts 13:15, 30
Acts 13:39, 9
Acts 15:8–9, 17
Acts 15:11, 26
Acts 16:1, 12
Acts 17:4, 12
Acts 17:12, 12
Acts 17:34, 12
Acts 18:8, 12
Acts 18:27, 12
Acts 20:24, 46, 51
Acts 26:22–23, 51

ROMANS

Romans 2:6–13, 9, 28, 47
Romans 2:13, 8, 28
Romans 3:21, 50
Romans 3:21–22, 12
Romans 3:22, 50
Romans 3:24–26, 5
Romans 3:25–26, 50
Romans 3:28, 28
Romans 4:5, 9
Romans 4:6–8, 48
Romans 4:24–35, 5
Romans 5:1, 8
Romans 5:9, 42
Romans 5:17, 17
Romans 6:16, 46
Romans 6:23, 17
Romans 10:3, 6
Romans 10:5, 13, 17
Romans 10:6, 13
Romans 10:9, 22
Romans 11:5, 14
Romans 11:6, 13, 14
Romans 11:26–27, 43, 44
Romans 11:28, 14
Romans 11:11–13, 42
Romans 12:5, 42

1 CORINTHIANS

1 Corinthians 6:11, 43
1 Corinthians 6:15, 45
1 Corinthians 6:16, 46
1 Corinthians 6:17, 45

SCRIPTURE INDEX

1 Corinthians 12:27, 45
1 Corinthians 15:1–4, 17
1 Corinthians 15:2–4, 13
1 Corinthians 15:11, 12
1 Corinthians 15:22, 42

2 CORINTHIANS

2 Corinthians 1:22, 17, 25
2 Corinthians 5:2–4, 43
2 Corinthians 5:17, 45

GALATIANS

Galatians 2:16, 12, 15
Galatians 2:21, 13
Galatians 3:8, 49
Galatians 3:11, 47
Galatians 3:12, 17
Galatians 3:21, 9, 47
Galatians 3:23, 49
Galatians 3:26, 44
Galatians 3:28, 46
Galatians 4:4–5, 23

EPHESIANS

Ephesians 1:7, 42
Ephesians 1:12, 12, 26
Ephesians 1:12–13, 12
Ephesians 1:13, 17, 25, 42, 46
Ephesians 1:22–23, 42
Ephesians 2:8, vii, 14
Ephesians 2:8–9, 50
Ephesians 2:13, 42
Ephesians 4:8–9, 18
Ephesians 4:9, 27
Ephesians 4:30, 17, 25, 46
Ephesians 5:26, 43

PHILIPPIANS

Philippians 3:9, 13
Philippians 3:20, 42

COLOSSIANS

Colossians 1:14, 42
Colossians 2:11–12, 25, 42

1 THESSALONIANS

1 Thessalonians 1:10, 46
1 Thessalonians 5:9, 42

2 THESSALONIANS

2 Thessalonians 2, 35

2 TIMOTHY

2 Timothy 2:15, vii, 4, 31

TITUS

Titus 3:5, 43

HEBREWS

Hebrews 2:1, 32
Hebrews 2:3, 32
Hebrews 3:6, 32
Hebrews 3:14, 32, 45
Hebrews 4:1, 32
Hebrews 4:1–14, 33
Hebrews 4:9, 44
Hebrews 4:9–11, 32
Hebrews 5:9, 32
Hebrews 6, 33, 34
Hebrews 6:1–8, 45
Hebrews 6:4–12, 32, 45
Hebrews 6:5–6, 37
Hebrews 6:6, 45
Hebrews 9:25–26, 23
Hebrews 10:4, 19, 51
Hebrews 10:22–26, 33
Hebrews 10:23–27, 32
Hebrews 10:26, 33
Hebrews 10:39, 37
Hebrews 11, 12, 27
Hebrews 12:14–15, 32

JAMES

James 1:1, 28, 50
James 1:21, 44
James 2:14–26, 32
James 2:19, 13
James 2:21, 50
James 2:24, 28, 43
James 5:8–9, 32
James 5:12, 33

1 PETER

1 Peter 1:10, 51
1 Peter 1:18–19, 43
1 Peter 1:18–20, 19
1 Peter 1:19–20, 24
1 Peter 1:20, 23

2 PETER

2 Peter 2:5, 25
2 Peter 3:16, 28

1 JOHN

1 John1:7, 43
1 John 3:7, 6, 10

3 JOHN

3 John 6, 53

JUDE

Jude 5, 25

REVELATION

Rev. 1:3, 33
Rev. 1:5, 43
Rev. 2:7, 33, 34
Rev. 2:11, 33, 34, 38
Rev. 2:17, 33, 34
Rev. 2:26, 33, 34
Rev. 3:7–13, 2
Rev. 3:3, 33
Rev. 3:5, 33
Rev. 3:11–12, 33
Rev. 3:21, 33
Rev. 7, 46
Rev. 7:14, 42
Rev. 11:7, 36
Rev. 12:2, 45
Rev. 12:11, 36, 37, 38
Rev. 12:17, 33, 34, 35
Rev. 13:8, 22, 24
Rev. 14, 46
Rev. 14:1, 44
Rev. 14:6, 32, 46
Rev. 14:11, 41, 45
Rev. 14:12, 33, 34, 35
Rev. 14:13, 45

Rev. 15:3, 32
Rev. 17:8, 23
Rev. 19:7–9, 42
Rev. 19:8, 43
Rev. 20:4, 36, 38, 44
Rev. 20:14, 38
Rev. 21:9–10, 41
Rev. 21:24, 25
Rev. 22:14, 33, 34, 38, 39

Printed in Great Britain
by Amazon